NGOVULA MBISI Jeancy

Behind the technology, computer science

NGOVULA MBISI Jeancy

Behind the technology, computer science

Virtual museum, computer science

ScienciaScripts

Imprint

Cover image: www.ingimage.com

This book is a translation from the original published under ISBN 978-620-2-28127-0.

Publisher:
Sciencia Scripts
is a trademark of
Dodo Books Indian Ocean Ltd. and OmniScriptum S.R.L publishing group

120 High Road, East Finchley, London, N2 9ED, United Kingdom
Str. Armeneasca 28/1, office 1, Chisinau MD-2012, Republic of Moldova, Europe
Managing Directors: Ieva Konstantinova, Victoria Ursu
info@omniscriptum.com

Printed at: see last page
ISBN: 978-620-8-50407-6

FOREWORD

In an ever-changing world, where technology is shaping our daily lives at a breathtaking pace, it is essential to understand not only the tools we use, but also the science behind these innovations. Behind the Technology: Computer Science and the Virtual Museum explores the fascinating intersection between computer science and the creation of virtual museums. The virtual museum represents a significant advance in the way we interact with art, culture and history. Thanks to digital technologies, these exhibition spaces transcend geographical and temporal boundaries, offering unprecedented access to precious collections and immersive experiences. However, behind this seductive façade lies a complex set of scientific and technical principles that deserve to be examined.

This book by ***NGOVULA MBISI Jeancy*** *invites readers to delve into the heart of computer science, revealing the algorithms, data structures and information systems that power these virtual museums. It is an exploration of virtual reality, artificial intelligence and data management technologies, and their impact on the way we perceive and understand cultural heritage. Contributions from experts in computer science, museology and interactive design enrich this analysis, offering varied perspectives on how virtual museums can not only preserve our heritage, but also make it accessible and engaging for future generations. Reading through these pages, readers will discover how computer science is transforming the museum experience and how, through technology, we can better understand our collective history. This book is an invitation to reflect on the role of technology in preserving and disseminating culture, while celebrating the innovation that makes these achievements possible.*

Professor LUTONADJO

DEDICATION

To Almighty God, Creator of Heaven and Earth, Master of time and circumstance;

To my very dear Parents: Joseph NGOVULA BAMENGA and Marie KATUNDA MANGALA ;

To my brothers and sisters: Glodie NGOVULA, Christelle NGOVULA, Saint-Pierre NGOVULA, Josué NGOVULA, Jephté NGOVULA for their love.

THANK YOU

We would like to take this opportunity to thank all those who have contributed in any way to this work.

We would first like to thank the academic authorities at ISTM/Kikwit for their support.

We would like to thank Professor ***Faustin MUSWAY DOUDOU****, who accepted to supervise this work despite his busy schedule.*

We would also like to thank Associate Professors ***MUZIAZIA LUPEMBA Jacques and IMBWELE KAFUTI Guy*** *for agreeing to supervise us despite their multiple occupations. Their advice and guidance were a great help.*

We would like to thank Professor LUTONADIO for agreeing to preface this manual.

Our thanks go straight to Dr Albert KIKONZI, Head of Research, who really helped us with the publication of this scientific work. Thank you very much, Doctor Albert.

We would like to express our gratitude to the scientific and teaching staff of ISETAM/Kikwit, ISTM/Kikwit, ISSS-E/Kikwit, the administrative staff and the workers.

We would also like to thank our friends who have encouraged us to continue our scientific research.

We would like to express our gratitude to all those whose names do not appear on this page.

NGOVULA MBISI Jeancy

BEHIND THE TECHNOLOGY, THE SCIENCE COMPUTING

Jeancy NGOVULA MBISI

Assistant 1 at the Institut Supérieur des Techniques Médicales in Kikwit

ABSTRACT Among the general public, and even in relatively well-informed circles, computing is still rarely perceived as a science, beyond its technical aspects. Given the growing importance of computing and digital technology in the economy and society in general, this is a regrettable state of affairs. It leads to a poor perception of the nature and impact of computer science research, and to a lack of interest among young people in studying this discipline, despite the fact that it creates jobs.

How can this trend be reversed? We believe that a presentation of computer science in the context of a virtual museum can make a contribution in two ways: (1) by showing that applications that are well known to everyone are based on fundamental concepts that form the basis of a rigorous approach to design and quality assurance; (2) by showing how these concepts have evolved over the course of history. A virtual presentation, with the flexibility and interactivity it allows, seems well suited to these objectives.

KEYWORDS: virtual museum, computer science

I. INTRODUCTION

The current image of IT is too often reduced to that of a technique. There are several reasons for this. The 'digitisation of the world', which is evident in almost all areas of everyday life, paradoxically contributes to this situation by giving the image of a collection of advances that are certainly spectacular, but which are reduced to their immediately perceptible technological aspect and highlighted by the media. The absence, until now, of computer science among the subjects taught at secondary level only reinforces this view. Finally, it should be noted that this reluctance to admit the existence of a computer science is not confined to the general public: we had to wait until 2003 for computer science to finally enter the Académie des Sciences in the form of a 'Mechanical and Computer Sciences' section, 2009 for a 'Computer Science and Digital Sciences' chair to be created at the Collège de France and 2012 for computer science to enter secondary school as a discipline in its own right. This situation is damaging, and there are several reasons for trying to change it.

- The growing role of digital technology in the economy and society means that broad public information on all aspects of this field;
- Innovation in new technologies, the engine of growth, relies on mastery of IT and digital sciences, and therefore on the quality of research in these disciplines; we need to help raise awareness of the nature and importance of this research;
- The crisis in scientific vocations among young people (and especially young girls) particularly affects computer science, a field where many skilled jobs are waiting to be filled. A better understanding of what computer science is, the type of activities that can be carried out in it and its relationship with the other sciences could change this attitude.

In this article, we propose one approach, among others, to help raise awareness of computing as a science. This effort is part of a more global movement to improve the public's scientific culture, which is currently the subject of numerous initiatives.

We propose to introduce the scientific aspects of computing within the framework of a virtual museum (Aconit, 2000) devoted to all aspects of this discipline. Far from an ex cathedra presentation, we believe that the starting point should be the objects and applications familiar to the public in an attempt to explain the scientific concepts underlying them. We also believe that the organisation of a virtual museum, with the multiplicity of viewpoints and the interactivity it allows, is well suited to an attractive presentation. In the remainder of this article, we first present the principles of a museum approach to computer science. We then use examples to show how these principles can be applied at different levels of understanding. Finally, we outline a historical approach to the development of computer science concepts and techniques.

II. INTRODUCING COMPUTER SCIENCE: PRINCIPLES OF A MUSEUM APPROACH

How can a museum of computing contribute to a better understanding of computing as a science? To answer this question, we first need to look at what computer science is. The purpose of computing is to process information. The technical side of computing is concerned with carrying out this processing using automated procedures. The science on which this processing is based comprises four fundamental concepts (Dowek, 2011): information, algorithm, machine and language. These concepts must be taken in a broad sense: a 'machine' is not necessarily a computer, but can be any device capable of carrying out actions according to a defined modus operandi: examples are a robot, a network, even a virtual machine (a real machine hidden under a layer of software), or quite simply an abacus.

A science is not defined solely by its object and its concepts; it is also identified by its approach and the methods it uses. From this point of view, computer science occupies an original place among the sciences (Dowek, 2012). The computer science approach (Wing, 2008) is characterised, among other things, by the central role of abstraction and decomposition, by the separation of concerns, by modelling and analysis, and by the complementarity and interaction between theory and experience. The term 'digital sciences' is used to describe the transformation of many disciplines through the adoption of the computer science approach and the conceptual and technical tools associated with it. physics, chemistry, biology, economics and linguistics, to name but a few, are all taking on a new face. More generally, society as a whole is becoming 'digital' as a result of the widespread use of IT objects and applications in everyday activities.

How can computer science be introduced through a museum approach? An abstract presentation ex abrupto is unlikely to attract attention. On the contrary, you need to start with concepts that are familiar to visitors: computer objects, which are now ubiquitous, and applications, which are widely known. Who hasn't used a mobile phone, consulted information on the web or used a computer? shop online? And even the user of a car or a simple washing machine runs computer programmes without its knowledge. We have therefore opted for an inductive approach. Starting with an application or an everyday object, we take visitors behind the scenes to identify the main basic concepts. We then demonstrate the universality of these concepts, and the fact that they underpin a variety of objects and situations. And we invite visitors who wish to go a little further by helping them to discover, again on the basis of familiar concepts, how the proper functioning (efficiency, availability, security) of an IT object or application is ensured.

In the following sections, we show some examples of the application of this approach. We believe that the use of the virtual (a concept widely developed within IT) offers many advantages (Aconit, 2000) for the development of presentations: flexibility of implementation, diversity of points of view and pathways, and the ability to adapt to the expectations and needs of users.
A computer museum can play a key role in the understanding of computing as a science. Here are a few ways in which it can contribute to this understanding:

1. Interactive Exhibitions

- **Hands-on involvement**: Interactive exhibits allow visitors to experiment with IT concepts in a fun way. For example, there are stations where visitors can code mini-programmes or manipulate robots.
- **Active learning**: This encourages active learning, where visitors can see the immediate results of their actions, reinforcing understanding.

2. Stories and Contexts

- **Narrating the History of Computing**: Presenting the evolution of computing through historical objects, from ancient machines to modern technologies, helps visitors understand the advances and challenges encountered over time.

• **Key figures**: Highlighting pioneers of computing and their contributions helps to personalise the history of science and inspire visitors.

3. Education and awareness

• **Workshops and Conferences**: Organising workshops, conferences and educational events on a variety of subjects (programming, cybersecurity, artificial intelligence) helps to deepen visitors' knowledge.

• **Collaboration with schools**: School programmes can be put in place in place to introduce young people to computers from an early age.

4. Exploring Practical Applications

• **Concrete examples**: Presenting concrete applications of IT in various fields (medicine, art, social sciences) helps to illustrate its impact on everyday life.

• **Collaborative projects**: Encourage collaborative projects where visitors can create solutions to real problems using technology.

5. Emerging Technologies

• **Advanced Technology Demonstrations**: Highlighting emerging technologies such as artificial intelligence, augmented reality and blockchain shows how IT is evolving and shaping our world.

• **Ethical exploration**: Discussing the ethical issues associated with these technologies (such as privacy and security) helps to develop critical thinking skills in visitors.

6. Information accessibility

• **Digital resources**: Offering online resources and virtual tours allows visitors to explore the museum and access additional information at their own pace

• **Multimedia**: Use videos, podcasts and articles to enrich the learning experience and reach a wider audience.

When introducing computer science into a museum approach, it is essential to structure the concepts in an accessible and engaging way. Here are some key principles for integrating these concepts into a virtual museum:

1. Interactivity and Engagement

• **Principle**: Encourage visitors to interact with the content.
• **Application**: Using interactive elements such as quizzes, educational games or simulations that allow users to explore IT concepts while discovering exhibits.

2. Visual Storytelling

• **Concept**: Use visuals to tell stories about the objects on display.
• **Application**: Create animations or computer graphics that explain computing concepts in relation to art objects or artefacts. For example, illustrate how a digital work of art is created using programming languages.

3. Contextualisation

• **Principle**: Link computer science to other disciplines.
• **Application**: Present works of art that incorporate technology, such as interactive installations, and explain how they use computer concepts (algorithms, networks, etc.).

4. Accessibility and Inclusiveness

• **Principle**: Make the museum accessible to all visitors.
• **Application**: Integrate accessibility features, such as subtitles for videos and audio descriptions, so that everyone can understand the IT concepts presented.

5. Education and awareness

• **Principle**: Educate the public about the importance of computer science.
• **Application**: Organise online workshops or webinars on IT topics such as cybersecurity or web development, linked to the works on display.

6. Use of Data

• **Principle**: Show how data can be used to enrich the museum experience.

• **Application**: To illustrate the analysis of museum attendance data to adapt exhibitions in real time or to personalise the user experience.

7. Emerging Technologies

• **Principle**: Integrate modern technologies into the museum experience.
• **Application**: Using augmented reality (AR) or virtual reality (VR) to allow visitors to explore interactive environments or works of art from different angles.

III. INTRODUCING COMPUTER SCIENCE: IMPLEMENTATION

To illustrate the approach we wish to apply, we will show how to identify some basic notions of computer science from the presentation, in the context of the virtual museum, of a common application. This illustrative example, although simplified, necessarily has a technical character which may make it difficult for a non-specialist reader to access. This is why, as a preamble to its description, we give a summarised explanation in more accessible terms. The chosen application is an online sales site; the reasons for this choice are explained below. The first stage of our approach can be summarised as follows:

- We describe a simplified version of the application and the hardware configuration on which it is implemented, in the form of a set of components whose functions and interactions we explain;
- We show how to give a simpler idea of this still relatively complex structure, through an abstract view of the processing of requests from a single client; this allows us to introduce abstraction (and its complement, refinement) as an intellectual tool for mastering the complexity of constructed systems.

Based on an analysis of the organisation and operation of the application, we have identified a number of basic concepts that we can use to describe this organisation and operation: information (the 'raw material'), the application itself, and the application itself. These include "knowledge support", algorithms (a scheme for processing information), databases (a way of organising information and a tool for accessing it), communication and interaction. Remember that we are describing here the explanatory approach we plan to follow in the virtual museum. At this stage, we have introduced We then show that these concepts are generic in nature, by applying them to the description of various computer science objects and applications. We then show that these concepts are generic in nature, by applying them to the description of various computer science objects and applications. The second part (section 4) allows us to go further by showing, still in the context of the virtual museum, how to endow an application with the properties that make it effectively usable: validity (it does what it is supposed to do); performance (it does it efficiently); dependability (it can be trusted in all circumstances); ergonomics (it is well adapted to users' needs). We show that guaranteeing these properties is a difficult task that requires methods and tools based on scientific advances. This is a far cry from the image of empiricism and 'do-it-yourself' that is still often attached to the perception of IT product development, particularly among younger people.

We will now take a more technical look at our approach. Let's remember that the chosen application is that of an online sales site. There are several reasons for this choice.

- this type of application is widely used, and its interface with
is relatively simple and intuitive;

- The architecture of e-commerce sites has been studied and refined for many years, and its layout is well known.

- the application is simple enough for us to be able to explain the broad outlines of its creation in an understandable way, and complex enough to illustrate the main concepts we want to introduce.

Here are a few steps and key concepts to consider in order to identify some basic notions of computer science based on the presentation of a common application in the context of a virtual museum:

1. User Interface (UI) and User Experience (UX)

• **Notion**: The user interface refers to the way in which a user interacts with the application (buttons, menus, etc.), while the user experience focuses on the user's overall satisfaction when using the application.

• **Example**: Analyse how a virtual museum application presents and makes navigation intuitive.

2. Software Architecture

• **Notion**: The underlying structure of an application, including the software components and their interaction.
• **Example**: Discuss the use of databases to store information about works and servers to manage user requests.

3. Programming languages

• **Notion**: The tools that developers use to create software.
• **Example**: Identify the languages used (such as HTML, CSS, JavaScript for the front-end and Python, Ruby for the back-end) and their role in developing the application.

4. Data Management

• **Notion**: How data is collected, stored and retrieved.
• **Example**: Explain how the works are catalogued and how they are used. users can search for specific information.

5. Computer security

• **Notion**: Measures taken to protect users' data and privacy.
• **Example**: Illustrate techniques for securing connections and protecting users' personal information.

6. Accessibility

• **Notion**: The ability of software to be used by people with different abilities.
• **Example**: Show how the application ensures that it is accessible to disabled people (subtitles, keyboard navigation, etc.).

7. Networks and Connectivity

• **Notion**: The protocols and infrastructures that enable users to access the online application.

• **Example**: Discuss the importance of a stable Internet connection for the operation of a virtual museum.

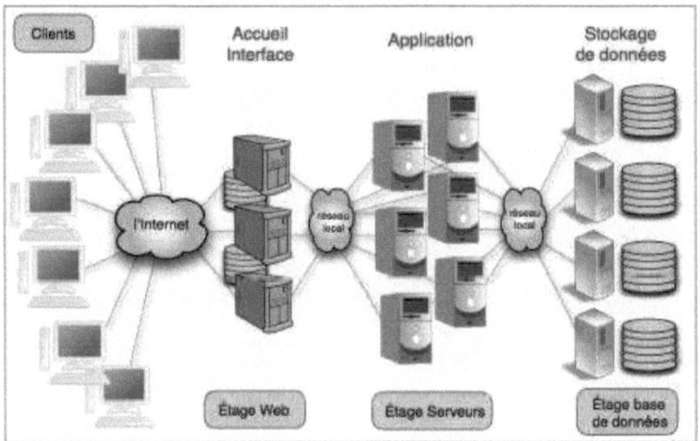

Figure 1: An e-commerce site

It is not our intention to describe a specific site, but a simplified generic model representative of e-commerce. Figure 1 shows both the hardware support and the general organisation of the application.

From left to right, the figure shows :

–the terminals that enable access to the server via the Internet; - the terminals that enable access to the server via the Internet; - the terminals that enable access to the server via the Internet.

the three floors of thc site :

- The web stage, which creates the interface presented to users and stores web pages that change relatively infrequently (typically, product catalogues for sale);

- The server floor, which implements the application itself, i.e. the various functions available to users (product and price searches, ordering, etc.), as well as the site's internal management (stock levels, price and product updates, etc.) ;

- The database stage, which stores all the information used by the application (stock levels, prices, customer files, etc.).

As you can see, each tier comprises a large number of physical components (computers, disk arrays), which guarantees both performance and site availability (as will be explained later).

This relatively complex physical view can be contrasted with a simpler abstract view, showing the flow of a request from a user (Figures 2 and 3).

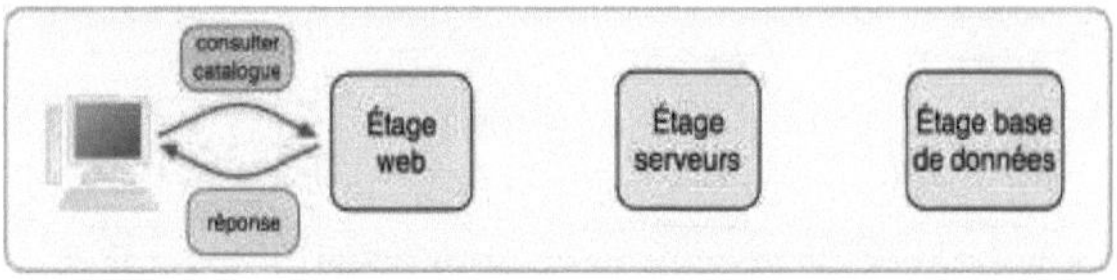

Figure 2: Consultation request path

Figure 2 shows the flow of a simple request (catalogue consultation) involving only the web stage. The diagram is that of a simple question-and-answer message exchange. Processing is reduced to searching for catalogue pages in local files. Figure 3 shows the processing of a purchase request for a particular user[1] . This time, the request message passes between the different levels, each of which is the site of specific processing: management of the interface in the web level, processing of the order in the application level, including interaction with the storage level for consulting and updating data (drawing up the invoice, stock management). There is also interaction with the physical world to launch delivery operations for the products ordered (whose availability has been checked beforehand), for payment of the purchase, and for any restocking. In the context of the museum, these operations are presented in the form of animations, with the necessary explanations. To integrate interaction with the physical world into a virtual museum, it's a good idea to present delivery, payment and restocking operations in the form of animations. Here's how to structure these elements, with explanations:

1. Launch of delivery operations

• **Animation**: Show a process where a user completes an order in the application. The animation can illustrate an interface where the user selects a product, confirms availability and then triggers the delivery operation.

• **Explanation**:

○ **Availability check**: Explain how the system queries the database to ensure that the product is in stock.

○ **Delivery Logistics**: Present how information is sent to a delivery service, and show an animated map of a delivery driver picking up the product.

2. **Payment Process**

• **Animation**: Illustrate the payment steps with visuals of a user filling in payment information on a secure interface.

• **Explanation**:

○ **Transaction security**: Describe the security protocols (such as encryption) used to protect credit card data.

○ **Payment Confirmation**: Shows how the system sends a confirmation to the customer and the warehouse.

3. **Product replenishment**

• **Animation**: Animate the process where a product is flagged as requiring replenishment, with alerts sent to managers.

• **Explanation**:

○ **Stock Management**: Explain how the system monitors stock levels and sends automatic notifications for replenishment.

○ **Interaction with the supplier**: Illustrate how orders are placed with suppliers, showing an interface where an employee validates the order.

4. Integration of the Elements

• **Interactivity**: Offer users the option of clicking on different elements of the animation to find out more about each stage (for example, click on the delivery person for details of the logistics).

• **Visual feedback**: Use graphs and indicators to show the progress of each operation (for example, a progress bar during payment).

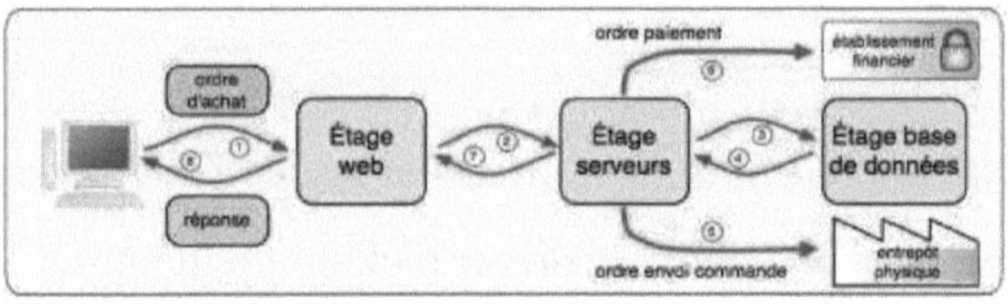

Figure 3: Path of a purchase request

How are scientific concepts now introduced? Here's how it works.

- The transition from Figure 1 to Figures 2 and 3 illustrates the notion of **abstraction** [2] an intellectual operation that plays a central role in computing.

We show that a complex reality can be modelled by a simple abstract diagram, on which we can usefully reason. Once the logical schema of actions has been defined at this level, a **refinement** stage enables it to be translated into actual operations performed by physical machines. If necessary, additional levels are introduced to facilitate the task. In this way, the refinement is carried out in 'magnifying glass' views of the different parts of the system, with increasingly high levels of magnification, with the implementation details specified at increasingly fine levels.

- The processing of a request is shown as a sequence of elementary actions, each triggered by the previous one. These actions follow a pre-established programme, but may include variations depending on the situation (such as processing the case where an item requested is unavailable). Here we find all the ingredients of the notion of **algorithm**.

- The processing of data (catalogue, stocks, prices, invoices, etc.) introduces the concept of **information**, two aspects of which can be explained: the need for logical organisation (the customer address list, catalogue headings, etc.), and the need for a physical storage method to enable retention and access. By combining these two aspects, we naturally arrive at the notion of a **database**.

- Customer communication with the site, handled by the web stage, introduces the notion of **interaction** (illustrated here by the request-response diagram). This leads to the need for an **interface**, a concept that is intuitively familiar to all screen users. The principles of ergonomics are introduced at a later stage (see section 4). The application is achieved by the collaboration of various components: the three stages, and within each of them, its various logical and physical components. This introduces the notion of **communication**, the logical aspects of which (request and response messages) can be distinguished from the physical aspects (transmission over networks). This brings us back to the notion of abstraction, developed elsewhere in the museum in relation to communication protocols and the operation of the Internet. We have therefore presented, in an intuitive way, some important notions of computer science. It can then be shown that these concepts, introduced on the basis of a specific example, are widely applicable to the general understanding of the functioning of a wide range of objects and applications. Examples of this are :

- A computer,

- A mobile phone,

- A robot,

- A video game,

- A standard web application, such as Google, - the web itself, in as an application support.

Visitors wishing to delve deeper into the subject can then move on to a more systematic presentation of the basic concepts of computer science: information, algorithm, machine, language, each of which is developed using examples. We will not go into detail here about the organisation of this presentation. The principle of dealing with the historical aspect (how these concepts gradually emerged) is described in section 5.

IV. GOING FURTHER: MAKING A APPLICATION USABLE

Building a usable[3] system is not enough. You need to guarantee that it has a number of properties:

- Validity (does the system do what is asked of it?),
- Efficiency (does it do it quickly, using few resources?),
- Operational reliability (does the system provide its service in all circumstances?),
- Ergonomics (is it adapted to users' needs and expectations?).

We wish to put across two ideas: these properties will not manifest themselves 'on their own' if they are not dealt with explicitly; guaranteeing them is a difficult undertaking which requires the help of the most advanced tools, both conceptual and technical. The first idea is probably not new to a public familiar with the malfunctions of the products and services they use (transport, household appliances, etc.). The second, on the other hand, emphasises the great complexity of IT objects, which means that the difficulties encountered in making them usable are still a long way from being mastered. Take the example of **validity**: the system must do "what we want it to do "And nothing else. But you still have to define "what you want it to do", and that's not so easy. Natural language, which is still often used, is not suited to this task because it is imprecise and ambiguous. So we have to invent a formalism: a model, a specification language, graphical tools, and so on. Once the specification problem has been solved (and this is not always the case), the next step is to ensure that the product conforms to the specification. Here again, there are various approaches: testing, reasoned construction, proof, each of which has its own field of application and, above all, its limitations. While we are still a long way from a general solution, significant advances have been made, all of which are based on solid scientific foundations: model checking, abstract interpretation, proof assistants, of which we can only give an approximate idea because they involve advanced concepts. On the other hand, we can point to examples of failed systems that were widely publicised by the media at the time (the failure of Ariane 501, the Pentium bug, and others), where it was shown after the event that the application of rigorous methods could have ensured their validity.

Efficiency relates to the quantitative aspects of a system's performance: response time, space occupied, stability of performance, etc. It is a quality that is very directly felt by users. Guaranteeing performance depends above all on the characteristics of the hardware components used (speed, storage capacity, etc.), but also on the application of appropriate design methods (shortening circuits, making good use of available information, etc.) and on the use of sophisticated modelling tools such as probabilistic models or queuing networks. These efficiency problems will also be illustrated in everyday applications: online sales sites, video games, computers, Google, etc.

Dependability ensures that a system performs its mission "to the best of its ability" in all circumstances, including unforeseen events such as failures, peak loads or malicious attacks. The public is increasingly aware of the problems of breakdowns, viruses, breaches of confidentiality, identity theft and other undesirable situations. Here again, a scientific approach is beginning to produce results, even if we are still a long way from mastering all the problems. We can point to a number of advances such as public key cryptography, watermarking techniques, reasoned use of redundancy and adaptive systems.

In the museum, these aspects will be illustrated by examples of well-known systems such as the Internet, Google, critical embedded systems, etc. The example of the online sales site, presented above, will be used to illustrate the notion of transaction, an (invisible) tool widely used in all consumer applications, as well as the use of redundancy to ensure service availability.

Ergonomics - adapting the system to the needs and expectations of users - is undoubtedly one of the aspects with which the public is most familiar. Here again, there is no shortage of counter-examples. We will highlight a few design principles that are often violated: the choice of the 'right' default options based on the expectations expressed; uniformity (similar presentation and actions for similar functions); the judicious re-use of available information; predictability, etc.

To conclude this section, we adopt the same inductive approach to the aspects studied here as we did for the introduction of the basic concepts. What remains to be done is to adapt the mode of presentation to the variety of situations just mentioned.

V.A HISTORICAL APPROACH

How did the concepts introduced so far gradually emerge? One approach to understanding concepts is to look at the history of their development. This historical view has several advantages:

- It highlights the context in which a particular conceptual or technical innovation emerged, whether in response to a need, following a stroke of genius, or as the crystallisation of ideas still 'in the air';

- It shows the stages of evolution from the earliest times to the present day, and raises questions about future developments. Two aspects of evolution are of particular interest to us:

- The relationships and interactions between the scientific aspects, technical, industrial and societal aspects of IT,

- The story of the dead ends, the wrong turns, the missed opportunities, which is just as instructive as that of the advances and successes.

- In this respect, we can illustrate different ways in which knowledge and techniques have advanced: foresight of changing needs, the ability to capture and give concrete form to unformulated ideas, or on the contrary, a radical break with the current way of thinking, and so on.

Without going into too much detail, we will illustrate the historical approach using the following examples two schematic examples of the routes planned within the virtual museum

A first example is the notion of **algorithm**, a central concept in computer science. The first algorithms appeared when an attempt was made to rigorously describe a method of operation (initially, a calculation) of a generic nature. One of the earliest known algorithms is that invented by Euclid around 300 BC to calculate the greatest common divisor of two integers. This example is particularly interesting because the answer to the two questions that are still relevant today for any algorithm (does it finish? does it give the expected result?) is formulated in elementary terms that can be understood by a secondary school pupil. An important figure is the Arab mathematician and astronomer al-Khwarismî, who in the 800s was the first to approach the study of algorithms (a term derived from his name) in a systematic way. Although many algorithms were subsequently invented and described, especially in the field of mathematics, it was not until the 1930s and the creation of metamathematics by Godel, Church, Kleene, Turing and others that the notion of algorithm was rigorously defined and the undecidability of the termination problem was established. Current work focuses on the problems of systematic construction and proof of algorithms, and major advances have been made in recent years (proof of complex systems such as a processor, a compiler or an operating system kernel).

A second example concerns the notion of a **programming language**, a way of expressing an algorithm for a machine (which may be physical or abstract). The history of languages is particularly rich (there are thousands of languages, of which only a few dozen have had a lasting life), and it is very instructive to show the motivations that have led to the various advances, as well as the considerations, not always rational, that have led to the success or abandonment of a particular language.

These two examples illustrate perfectly the importance of the scientific substrate, often ignored or underestimated, which is at the root of concrete advances of considerable practical importance. Many other paths are just as instructive in this respect (machines, information, databases, networks, robotics, etc.). A virtual information museum works by using digital technologies to offer a remote exploration and learning experience. Here are some key elements of how it works:

1. **Online platform**: Virtual museums are generally accessible via websites or mobile applications. They allow users to access collections, exhibitions and educational resources from anywhere.

2. **Digital exhibitions**: Objects and works of art are often presented in the form of high-quality photos, videos, detailed descriptions and sometimes interactive virtual tours that simulate a physical visit.

3. **Interactivity**: Users can interact with content, for example by zooming in on works of art, browsing galleries, or taking part in quizzes and educational games.

4. **Accessibility**: These museums give a wider public access to culture and education, regardless of their geographical location or physical ability.

5. **Online events and activities**: Many virtual museums offer live lectures, workshops and guided tours, allowing real-time interaction with experts.

6. **Educational resources**: They often offer educational resources for teachers and students, such as lesson plans and collection-based activities.

In short, a virtual information museum uses technology to democratise access to culture and enrich the learning experience.

VI. THE IMPORTANCE OF VIRTUAL MUSEUMS

VI.1. Infrastructure Technical

• **Servers and Hosting**: The need for robust servers to manage traffic and store large quantities of data, particularly large multimedia files.

• **Bandwidth**: A fast and stable Internet connection is essential to ensure smooth access to content, particularly for immersive experiences.

VI.2. Digitalisation of Collections

• **Digitisation quality**: Objects must be digitised at high resolution to preserve detail. This requires high-quality equipment and technical skills.

• **Interoperability of formats**: The various file formats (images, videos, 3D) must be compatible with each other and with the museum's management systems.

VI.3. 3D Modelling and Virtual Reality

• **Complexity of Modelling**: Creating realistic, interactive 3D models requires skills in graphics and modelling, as well as specialist software.

• **Device Compatibility**: Ensuring that virtual reality experiences work on a variety of devices (VR headsets, computers, mobiles) can be a technical challenge.

• **Creating 3D models**: Using modelling software such as Blender or SketchUp to create realistic representations of objects.

• **Virtual Reality (VR) and Augmented Reality (AR)**: Developing immersive experiences where users can explore exhibitions interactively.

VI.4. Accessibility and Inclusiveness

• **Universal design**: Developing an interface that is accessible to everyone, including people with disabilities, requires particular attention to design and implementation.

• **Languages and Localisation**: Offering content in several languages and adapting interfaces for different audiences is a logistical and technical challenge.
• **Democratising culture**: Virtual museums allow a global audience to access collections without the constraints of geography, particularly for those who cannot visit physical museums because of distance or disability.
• **24/7 availability**: They offer constant access to resources, enabling users to visit exhibitions at any time.

VI.5. Content Management Systems (CMS)

• **Selecting the CMS**: Choose a system that is adapted to the museum's specific needs, capable of managing varied collections and offering customisation options.
• **Updates and Maintenance**: Ensuring that the CMS is regularly updated for reasons of security and functionality.

VI.6. Data security

• **Data protection**: Ensuring the security of user data and digital collections against hacking and data loss.
• **Copyright and Licensing**: Managing the copyright of works on display and ensure that the content used complies with current regulations.

VI.7. Commitment by Public

• **Interactivity and User Experience**: Creating engaging experiences that encourage visitors to explore and interact with the content requires thoughtful design.
• **Feedback and Evaluation**: Implement tools to gather user feedback and evaluate the effectiveness of virtual exhibitions.

VI.8. Education

• **Interactive learning tools**: Virtual museums offer educational resources that can be integrated into school curricula, providing engaging and interactive learning experiences.
• **Continuing education**: They facilitate lifelong learning by offering educational content to a wide range of audiences.

VI.9. Conservation

• **Digital preservation**: Digitising works of art and artefacts contributes to their conservation, reducing the risk of physical deterioration. It also makes it possible to preserve rare or fragile objects.
• **Documentation**: Virtual museums keep digital records of works, ensuring that they are accessible even if physical objects are damaged or lost.

VI. 1O. Promotion of Culture

By making collections accessible to everyone, virtual museums help to spread culture and heritage. They highlight artists, artistic movements and histories that may not be adequately represented in physical museums.

*VI.11.*Cost-effectiveness

The creation and management of a virtual museum can be less costly than that of a traditional museum. This saves on maintenance costs, staff and physical infrastructure, while reaching a wider audience.

*VI.12.*Reduction of Costs

• **Saving resources**: Virtual museums can reduce the running costs associated with maintaining a physical space, while reaching a wider audience.
• **Alternative business models**: These offer monetisation opportunities through subscriptions, donations or sales of digital by-products.

VII. TECHNICAL COMPONENTS OF A VIRTUAL MUSEUM

VII.1. Content Management Systems (CMS)

• **Choice of CMS**: Selection of a suitable platform for organising, managing and updating the museum's content, such as WordPress, Drupal or specific museum solutions.
• **Customisation**: Ability to adapt the CMS to meet the particular needs of the museum, including specific functionalities for interactivity.

VII.2. Interfaces User

• **Adaptive Design**: Developing accessible interfaces that adapt to different devices (computers, tablets, smartphones) and to the needs of users, including those with disabilities.
• **Multilingualism**: Integrating several languages to reach an international and diverse audience.

VII.3. Interactivity

• **Interactive elements**: Integration of quizzes, games and other interactive elements to engage visitors and enrich their experience.
• **Virtual Guided Tours**: Online sessions with experts to guide users through the collections.

VIII. IMMERSIVE EXPERIENCES IN A VIRTUAL MUSEUM

VIII.1. Modelling 3D

• **Creation of realistic models**: Using 3D modelling software to faithfully reproduce objects and works of art, allowing visitors to explore them from different angles.

• **Interactive navigation**: users can interact with the 3D models, zooming in, rotating or discovering specific details, offering total immersion in the work.

VIII.2. Virtual Reality (VR)

• **Immersive Virtual Tours**: Integration of virtual reality headsets to offer immersive tours, where users feel present in the museum environment.

• **Simulations and Reconstructions**: Creating simulation experiences that allow visitors to experience historical events or explore cultural environments in 3D.

VIII.3. Augmented Reality (AR)

• **Information Overlay** : Use of augmented reality applications that overlay additional information on physical objects when viewed through a mobile device.

• **Interactive experiences**: Users can interact with virtual elements in real time, enriching their understanding of the works on display.

VIII.4. Exhibitions Interactive

• **Participatory elements**: Integration of quizzes, games and other interactive elements that encourage visitors to take an active part in the experience.

• **Interactive Narration**: Use of interactive narratives that allow users to choose their own route through the exhibition, making each visit unique

VIII.5. Guided Tours Virtual

• **Live Sessions with Experts**: Organisation of guided tours in real time with curators or experts, allowing visitors to ask questions and obtain in-depth information.
• **Tour recordings**: Provision of pre-recorded guided tours that can be viewed at any time, offering flexibility to users.

VIII.6. Content Multimedia

• **Integration of Video and Audio**: Use of audiovisual media to enrich the experience, such as documentaries, expert interviews or audio commentaries on the works.
• **Slideshows and Galleries**: Presentation of collections through interactive slideshows that allow users to navigate easily between works.

IX. MANAGEMENT AND MAINTENANCE OF A VIRTUAL MUSEUM

IX.1. Content Management Systems (CMS)

•**Choice of CMS**: Selection of a suitable platform that enables content to be managed efficiently, such as WordPress, Drupal or museum-specific solutions. The CMS must be able to support various file formats and offer analysis tools.

•**Regular Updates**: Updating the CMS for security, performance and new features. This includes updating the plugins and themes used.

IX.2. Maintenance Technical

•**Performance Monitoring**: Use of tools to monitor site speed and performance, in order to quickly identify and resolve technical problems that could affect the user experience.

•**Regular back-ups**: Setting up an automatic back-up system to protect data and content against loss or technical failure.

IX.3. Management of Content

•**Content creation and updating**: Development of new content, such as articles, videos and exhibitions, to maintain visitor interest and enrich the experience offered.

•**Organisation of Collections**: Regular updating of collections and exhibitions, ensuring that information is accurate and easily accessible.

IX.4. Data security

•**Protection of Sensitive Data**: Implementation of security protocols to protect user information and sensitive data relating to collections.

•**Copyright Management**: Ensuring compliance with copyright and intellectual property regulations for works on display.

IX.5. Feedback and continuous improvement

• **User Feedback Collection**: Implementation of mechanisms to obtain feedback from visitors, for example using questionnaires or behavioural analysis tools.
• **Data analysis**: Use of analytics tools to assess user engagement, most visited pages, and other metrics to optimise the experience.

IX.6. Support Technical

• **User Support**: To provide technical support to help users navigate the platform, resolve technical problems and answer questions.
• **Staff training**: Ongoing staff training on new technologies, content management and best practice in security and user engagement.

X. RECOMMENDED PERFORMANCE ANALYSIS TOOLS FOR A VIRTUAL MUSEUM

Analysing the performance of a virtual museum is essential for understanding user engagement and optimising the experience. Here are some recommended tools:

X.1. Google Analytics

• **Description**: Free tool for tracking site traffic, user behaviour and conversions.
• **Features** :

○ Monitoring of page views, time spent on each page and bounce rate.
○ Analysis of traffic sources (organic search, social networks, etc.).
○ Creation of customised reports to evaluate specific campaigns or events.

X.2. Hotjar

• **Description**: Behavioural analysis tool that provides visual information on how users interact with the site.
• **Features** :

○ Heatmaps showing the areas clicked and scrolled by users.
○ Recording of user sessions to observe browsing patterns.
○ Integrated surveys and feedback to gather opinions directly from visitors.

X.3. Matomo (formerly Piwik)

• **Description** : Open source analysis platform offering total control over data.
• **Features** :
○ Real-time visitor tracking with detailed reports.
○ Respect for data confidentiality, which is crucial for many users.
○ Features advanced of segmentation and customisable reports.

X.4. Crazy Egg

• **Description**: Visualisation tool that helps to understand how users interact with the site.

• **Features** :

o Heat maps and session recordings.

o A/B testing tools to assess the impact of design changes.

o Reports on clicks, scrolls and interactions.

X.5. SEMrush

• **Description**: Primarily an SEO tool, but also offers site performance analysis functions.

• **Features** :

o Monitoring organic and paid search performance.

o Competitor and keyword analysis to optimise content.

o Site audit to identify technical problems affecting performance.

X.6. PageSpeed Insights

• **Description**: Google tool that analyses page loading speed and provides optimisation recommendations.

• **Features** :

o Analysis of performance on mobile and desktop.

o Suggestions for improving loading times, such as compressing images or minimising JavaScript.

X.7. Google Search Console

• **Description**: Google's free tool for monitoring your site's presence in search results.

• **Features** :

o Tracking of search performance and clicks.

- Identification of exploration errors and indexing problems.
- Reports on the keywords that generate traffic to the site.

A. The concept of a Museum of Computing and the Digital Society: is an exciting initiative that aims to explore the impact of computing and digital technologies on our society. Here are some key elements that might characterise such a museum:

1. **Thematic exhibitions**

- **History of computing**: Sections dedicated to the pioneers of computing, the first computers and major technological developments.
- **Emerging technologies**: Introducing the latest innovations such as artificial intelligence, virtual reality and the Internet of Things.

2. **Interactivity**

- **Interactive stations**: allowing visitors to experiment with technologies such as programming simulators or augmented reality demonstrations.
- **Workshops and seminars**: Offering educational programmes for all ages on subjects such as programming, cybersecurity and digital ethics.

3. **Collection of historical objects**

- **Computer hardware**: Exhibit iconic computers, retro video games and other technological devices.
- **Documents and archives**: Conserving archives of patents, publications and correspondence from key figures in computing.

4. **Reflecting on the impact on society**

- **Digital society**: Exploring how digital technologies are transforming work, communication, education and culture.
- **Ethical issues**: Addressing topics such as privacy, misinformation and the

environmental impact of technology.

5. Partnerships and Collaborations

- **Collaboration with universities and technology companies**: for temporary exhibitions and research projects.
- **Community events**: Organising hackathons, conferences and public discussions on digital issues.

B. The idea of a museum dedicated to computing and the digital society is particularly relevant in our increasingly connected world. Here are some aspects to consider when creating such a museum:

1. The Museum's objectives

- **Education**: Raising public awareness of digital technologies, their history and their impact on society.
- **Conservation**: Preserving historic IT-related objects, such as old computers, iconic software and communication devices.

2. Thematic exhibitions

- **History of Computing**: Exhibitions on the pioneers of computing, such as Alan Turing and Ada Lovelace, and technological milestones.
- **Evolution of Technologies**: An interactive timeline showing the evolution of computers, networks and mobile devices.
- **Societal impact**: Exploring how IT has transformed sectors such as education, health and communications.

3. Interactive Experiences

- **Simulations and Workshops**: Areas where visitors can code, experiment with old technologies, or take part in workshops on subjects such as cybersecurity.
- **Virtual Visits**: offering immersive online experiences, enabling a global

audience to discover the exhibitions.

4. Partnerships and Collaborations

- Collaborating with universities, technology companies and others cultural institutions to enrich the museum's content and resources.
- Organising conferences and seminars with experts in the field.

5. Accessibility and Inclusion

- Ensure that the museum is accessible to all, including people with disabilities.
- Offer content in several languages and adapted to different levels of understanding.

6. Sustainability

- To integrate sustainable practices into the management of the museum, using green technologies and raising public awareness of the environmental issues associated with IT.

C. A Museum ofComputing and the Digital Society would be a fascinating place dedicated to exploring the impact of digital technology on our society. Here are some ideas of what such a museum might include:

1. **Thematic exhibitions**

- **History of computing**: from ancient computers to modern technologies, with iconic objects such as the first personal computers, retro games consoles, etc.
- **Evolution of the Internet**: An interactive timeline showing the development of the web, from the first browsers to today's social networks.

2. **Interactive Installations**

- **Technological simulations**: installations that allow visitors to program simple algorithms or discover how operating systems work.

• **Virtual reality**: immersive experiences that illustrate concepts such as artificial intelligence and augmented reality.

3. **Education and awareness**

• **Workshops and conferences**: Educational events on subjects such as cybersecurity, personal data protection and the ethical challenges of AI.
• **Programmes for young people**: Initiatives to familiarise children and teenagers with programming and digital technologies.

4. **Exhibitions on the Digital Society**

• **Social impact of technology**: Case studies on how technology has transformed work, communication and leisure.

• **Digital Art**: A gallery dedicated to artists who use digital technologies as a means of expression.

5. **Conservation and Archives**

• **Preservation of digital heritage**: A section devoted to the preservation of software, historical websites and video games.

6. **Virtual Tours**

• Online access to enable people from further afield to discover the exhibitions and interact with the content, thereby enhancing accessibility.

D. Ensuring the long-term future of a digital museum requires a strategic, multi-dimensional approach. Here are some key elements to consider:

1. Sustainable Financial Support

• **Varied funding models**: Diversifying sources of income through grants, corporate partnerships, private donations and ticket sales for events.

• **Memberships and subscriptions**: Create membership programmes to build audience loyalty and generate recurring revenue.

2. Technology Update

• **Regular maintenance**: updating software and platforms to keep pace with the latest technologies.
• **Continuous innovation**: Integrating new technologies, such as augmented reality or artificial intelligence, to enhance the user experience.

3. Up-to-date and relevant content

• **Updating exhibitions**: Regularly updating content to reflect technological and social developments.
• **Partnerships with institutions**: Working with universities, researchers and other museums to enhance collections and exhibitions.

4. Accessibility and Inclusiveness

• **Accessible user interface**: Design an intuitive and accessible interface that takes into account the needs of disabled people.
• **Multilingual content**: Offer translations in several languages to reach a global audience.

5. Community involvement

• **Public feedback**: Encourage visitors to give their opinion and take part in content creation.
• **Events and workshops**: Organise regular activities to engage the community and attract new visitors.

6. Digital preservation

• **Data backup**: Implement backup systems to protect digital collections against data loss.

• **Archiving**: Developing archiving strategies to preserve works of art and long-term digital documents.

7. Promotion and Visibility

• **Digital marketing**: Using social networks, SEO and other digital marketing strategies to increase the museum's visibility.

E. Partnering with influencers and bloggers to reach new audiences. Ensuring the long-term future of a digital museum requires a strategic, multi-faceted approach. Here are a few key elements to consider:

1. **Sustainable Business Model**

• **Diversified funding**: Seek a variety of funding sources, including grants, corporate partnerships, private donations, and income generated by events or workshops.

• **Memberships and subscriptions**: Offer membership programmes or subscriptions that offer exclusive benefits to members.

2. **Quality Content**

• **Regular updating**: Ensuring that content and exhibitions are frequently updated to reflect technological developments and new trends.

• **Working with experts**: Working with specialists in the field to ensure the accuracy and relevance of the information presented.

3. **Accessibility and Inclusiveness**

• **Adapted User Interface**: Developing a user-friendly interface that is accessible to all users, including people with disabilities.

• **Multilingual content**: Offer content in several languages to reach an international audience.

4. **Community commitment**

• **Local Partnerships**: Working with schools, universities and community organisations to promote the museum and its activities.
• **Visitor feedback**: Gather regular feedback from users to improve the experience and meet their expectations.

5. **Technology and Infrastructure**

• **Robust platform**: invest in a reliable and secure technological infrastructure to avoid breakdowns and protect user data.
• **Adaptability to new technologies**: Be ready to integrate new technologies to stay relevant, such as virtual reality, artificial intelligence, or mobile applications.

6. **Communication Strategy**

• **Active Online Presence**: Maintain a strong presence on social networks and digital platforms to attract and engage audiences.
• **Marketing and Promotion**: Use marketing campaigns to publicise new exhibitions and events, targeting specific groups.

7. **Digital preservation**

• **Archiving**: Implementing archiving protocols to preserve digital content over the long term, using standard formats and backup systems.
• **Technological updates**: Plan regular updates and content migrations to avoid obsolescence.

F. Measuring the impact of a digital museum on its audience is essential for evaluating its success and improving its offerings. Here are several methods and indicators to consider:

1. **Web Traffic Statistics**

• **Visits and Unique Users**: Analyse the number of visits and unique users on the site to get an idea of the museum's reach.
• **Visit duration**: Measure the time spent on the site or on specific sections to assess visitor engagement.

2. **Interactivity and Engagement**

• **Interaction Rate**: Track users' interactions with content, such as clicks on exhibitions, downloads of resources or participation in games and quizzes.
• **Comments and feedback**: Gather visitor opinions via forms, surveys or social networks to understand their experience.

3. **Social Network Analysis**

• **Network engagement**: Measuring likes, shares, comments and mentions on social platforms to assess the impact and resonance of publications.
• **Community growth**: Observe changes in the number of followers and engagement over time.

4. **Evaluations and Surveys**

• **Post-visit surveys**: Send surveys to visitors after their experience to get feedback on what they liked or what they would like to see improved.
• **Content evaluations**: Ask users to evaluate the exhibitions or educational content to measure their satisfaction.

5. **Educational Impact**

• **Tests and evaluations** : For educational programmes, use pre- and post-assessments to measure participants' knowledge gains.
• **Workshop Participation Rate**: Track participation in events or workshops to assess interest and commitment.

6. **Partnerships and Collaborations**

• **Partner feedback**: Obtain feedback from educational institutions, cultural organisations or other partners on the impact of the collaboration.

7. **Case Studies and Testimonials**

• **Visitors' stories**: Collect visitors' stories to understand how the museum has influenced their understanding or appreciation of computing and digital technology.
• **Case studies**: Analyse specific user groups (students, families, professionals) to identify particular impacts.

8. **Monitoring Objectives**

• **Key Performance Indicators (KPIs)**: Define specific KPIs in line with the museum's objectives (e.g. increasing the number of visits, improving engagement, etc.) and monitor their progress.

G. Measuring the impact of a digital museum on its public requires a methodical and diversified approach. Here are some key methods and indicators to consider:

1. **Analysis of Usage Data**

• **Visit statistics**: Track the number of unique visitors, page views and average session length to assess engagement.
• **User behaviour**: analyse user navigation paths to identify the most popular sections and those that need improvement.

2. **Surveys and Feedback**

• **Online questionnaires**: Distribute surveys to gather feedback on user experience, content quality and visitor expectations.

• **Ratings and comments**: Allow users to leave ratings and comments on exhibitions and resources.

3. **Engagement on Social Networks**

• **Interaction**: Measure likes, shares, comments and the reach of publications to gauge public interest.

• **Analytical Sentiment**: Analyse the tone and sentiment of the comments to understand how the museum is perceived.

4. **Case Studies and Testimonials**

• **Visitor Stories**: Collecting testimonials and stories from visitors to illustrate the personal and educational impact of the museum.

• **Case studies**: Develop case studies on specific groups (schools, communities) to assess the impact on targeted populations.

5. **Educational Partnerships**

• **Feedback from Educators**: Work with teachers and educators to measure how the museum's resources are being used in school programmes.

• **Impact on learning**: Assess whether virtual visits improve understanding of specific subjects or skills.

6. **Monitoring Objectives**

• **Key Performance Indicators (KPIs)**: Define clear KPIs (e.g. visitor return rate, satisfaction rate) to measure the achievement of the museum's objectives.

• **Regular reporting**: Produce regular impact reports to monitor progress and adjust strategies accordingly.

7. **Accessibility assessment**

- **Accessibility analysis**: Assess whether the content is accessible to all, including people with disabilities, and measure the impact on these groups.

Ensuring the long-term future of a digital museum requires a strategic, multi-faceted approach. Here are some key elements to consider:

1. **Sustainable Business Model**

- **Diversified funding**: Seek a variety of funding sources, including grants, corporate partnerships, private donations, and income generated by events or workshops.
- **Memberships and subscriptions**: Offer membership programmes or subscriptions that offer exclusive benefits to members.

2. **Quality Content**

- **Regular updating**: Ensuring that content and exhibitions are frequently updated to reflect technological developments and new trends.
- **Working with experts**: Working with specialists in the field to ensure the accuracy and relevance of the information presented.

3. **Accessibility and Inclusiveness**

- **Adapted User Interface**: Developing a user-friendly interface that is accessible to all users, including people with disabilities.
- **Multilingual content**: Offer content in several languages to reach an international audience.

4. **Community commitment**

- **Local Partnerships**: Working with schools, universities and community organisations to promote the museum and its activities.
- **Visitor feedback**: Gather regular feedback from users

to improve the experience and meet their expectations.

5. **Technology and Infrastructure**

- **Robust platform**: invest in a reliable and secure technological infrastructure to avoid breakdowns and protect user data.
- **Adaptability to new technologies**: Be ready to integrate new technologies to stay relevant, such as virtual reality, artificial intelligence, or mobile applications.

6. **Communication Strategy**

- **Active Online Presence**: Maintain a strong presence on social networks and digital platforms to attract and engage audiences.
- **Marketing and Promotion**: Use marketing campaigns to publicise new exhibitions and events, targeting specific groups.

7. **Digital preservation**

- **Archiving**: Implementing archiving protocols to preserve digital content over the long term, using standard formats and backup systems.
- **Technological update**: Plan for regular updates and new technologies content migration to avoid obsolescence.

Measuring the impact of a digital museum on its audience is essential for evaluating its effectiveness and improving its offerings. Here are some key methods and indicators to consider:

1. **Web Data Analysis**

- **Visitors and engagement**: Use analysis tools (such as Google Analytics) to track the number of visitors, the time spent on the site, the most popular pages and the bounce rate.
- **User demographics**: analyse demographic data to better understand who is

visiting the museum (age, location, etc.) and adapt content accordingly.

2. **Polls and surveys**

• **Post-visit surveys**: Send surveys to visitors after their experience to gather information about their satisfaction, perceived impact and desired improvements.
• **Content evaluations**: Ask users to evaluate specific exhibitions or educational resources to measure engagement and impact.

3. **Qualitative feedback**

• **Testimonials and Reviews**: Encourage visitors to leave comments or testimonials about their experience, which can provide valuable insights.
• **Focus groups**: Organise focus groups with users to explore their perceptions and expectations.

4. **Monitoring Social Interactions**

• **Social Network Engagement**: Analysing likes, shares and comments on museum-related publications to assess public interest and interaction.
• **Mentions and Discussions**: Monitor mentions of the museum on social networks and in the media to understand its influence and reach.

5. **Learning Assessment**

• **Tests and quizzes**: Include quizzes or tests before and after the experience to measure the knowledge acquired by visitors.
• **Monitoring educational progress**: Working with schools to assess the museum's educational impact on pupils.

6. **Analysis of Visitor Behaviour**

• **User Journey Mapping**: Analyse how visitors navigate the site, which sections are the most popular, and where they abandon their visit.

- **Use of Resources**: Track downloads of educational resources, registrations for events or workshops, and other measurable interactions.

7. **Impact on the Community**

- **Partnerships and collaboration**: Evaluate collaborations with schools, universities or community organisations to measure the impact on awareness and education.
- **Participation in Events**: Measure audience engagement at online or face-to-face events associated with the museum.

H. Effective analysis of the qualitative data collected requires a systematic and structured approach. Here are some steps and methods to guide this analysis:

1. **Data preparation**

- **Transcription**: If the data is in the form of audio or video recordings, start by transcribing them. This will give you a clear text to analyse.
- **Organisation**: Group data by theme, response type or category to facilitate analysis.

2. **Getting to know the data**

- **Initial reading**: Read the data carefully several times to familiarise yourself with the content and identify any first impressions or emerging themes.

3. **Data coding**

- **Code creation**: Develop codes to categorise information. This can be done inductively (by letting themes emerge from the data) or deductively (using pre-established themes).
- **Use of software**: Consider using qualitative analysis software such as NVivo,

Atlas.ti or MAXQDA to facilitate the coding and organisation of data.

4. **Theme identification**

• **Emerging themes** : Examine codes to identify recurring or significant themes. Group similar codes together to form broader categories.
• **Diagrams and Mind Maps**: Use visualisations to represent the relationships between themes and codes, which can help clarify connections.

5. **Data interpretation**

• **Contextualisation**: Analyse the results taking into account the context in which the data was collected. What circumstances may have influenced the responses?
• **Search for Meaning**: Try to understand the meaning of the answers. What do they reveal about participants' perceptions, attitudes or behaviour?

6. **Validation of results**

• **Triangulation**: Compare the results of different data sources (for example, between surveys and interviews) to reinforce the credibility of the conclusions.
• **Feedback from participants**: If possible, go back to the participants to check that their feedback has been correctly interpreted.

7. **Report and presentation of results**

• **Structured writing**: Write a clear, structured report, incorporating direct quotes from participants to illustrate the themes identified.
• **Visualisations** : Use graphs, tables and diagrams to make your results more accessible and understandable.

8. **Use of Results**

• **Recommendations**: Formulate recommendations based on the results of the analysis to inform strategic decisions and improve the museum's offerings.
• **Follow-up**: Plan regular evaluations to see if the changes made in response to the qualitative data are having a positive impact.

I. Effective analysis of qualitative data requires a structured approach to extracting meaningful insights. Here are a few steps and methods to guide this analysis:

1. **Data Collection**

• **Varied formats**: Gather data from several sources, such as surveys, interviews, focus groups and online comments.
• **Transcription**: For interviews or discussions, transcribe the recordings to facilitate analysis.

2. **Immersion in Data**

• **In-depth reading**: Read all the answers carefully to familiarise yourself with the content and identify initial themes.
• **Note-taking**: Note down impressions, recurring ideas and points of interest during this exploration phase.

3. **Data coding**

• **Development of a Coding System**: Create codes (words or phrases) to represent the key themes or concepts identified in the responses.
• **Open coding**: Start with open coding, allowing the themes to emerge naturally from the text.
• **Axial coding**: group similar codes together to form broader categories for easier analysis.

4. **Theme identification**

• **Thematic analysis**: Identify the major themes emerging from the coded data. Look for recurring patterns or significant discrepancies.
• **Creating Mind Maps**: Visualise the relationships between themes and sub-themes to better understand connections.

5. **Data interpretation**

• **Contextualisation**: Analyse the results taking into account the context, the motivations of the respondents and the specific characteristics of the target audience.
• **Insights Extraction**: Identify significant insights that respond to the initial research questions or the museum's objectives.

6. **Validation of results**

• **Triangulation**: Comparing results with other sources of data (quantitative or qualitative) to check their validity.
• **Feedback from participants**: If possible, share the results with a few participants to get their feedback and confirm the interpretation.

7. **Results presentation**

• **Clear reports**: Write clear and concise reports that summarise the results, identified themes and recommendations.
• **Data visualisation**: Use graphs, tables and infographics to make results more accessible and attractive

8. **Follow-up and Actions**

• **Implementing the Recommendations**: Use the insights gained from the analysis to inform the museum's future decisions and strategies.
• **Ongoing evaluation**: Plan regular evaluations to measure the impact of the

changes implemented and adjust strategies accordingly.

Effective analysis of qualitative data requires a systematic approach to extracting valuable insights. Here are the key steps to follow:

1. **Data Collection**

• **Accurate recordings**: Make sure that data is well documented, whether through notes, audio or video recordings.
• **Representative sampling**: Choose a representative sample to capture a variety of perspectives.

2. **Transcription**

• **Transcribe recordings**: Convert all audio or video recordings into text for easy analysis.
• **Transcript check**: Reread transcripts to ensure accuracy and clarity.

3. **Data coding**

• **Development of a Coding System**: Create categories or themes based on research questions or emerging topics.
• **Open coding**: Identify initial codes by scanning the data without bias, then refine them into more specific codes.

• **Axial coding**: Link codes together to identify relationships and patterns.

4. **Thematic analysis**

• **Identifying Emerging Themes**: Group similar codes together to identify recurring themes or patterns in the data.
• **Documentation**: Note down specific examples to illustrate each theme identified.

5. **Data interpretation**

• **Context and meaning**: Analyse the themes in the light of their cultural, social and historical context to understand their meaning.
• **Critical reflection**: Be aware of your own biases and prejudices that could influence the interpretation.

6. **Validation**

• **Triangulation**: Compare the results of one source with other sources of data (quantitative or qualitative) to reinforce the credibility of the results.
• **Feedback**: Share preliminary results with participants or experts to obtain feedback on interpretations.

7. **Results presentation**

• **Clear reports**: Write reports that summarise the results in a clear and structured way, including direct quotes to illustrate the main points.
• **Visualisation**: Use diagrams or concept maps to visually represent the relationships between themes.

8. **Follow-up and Action**

• **Action Plan**: Develop recommendations based on the analysis to improve the museum's offerings and engagement.
• **Ongoing evaluation**: Set up an ongoing evaluation process to refine the analysis in the future.

J. Dealing with conflicting data during coding in qualitative analysis can be a challenge, but it is also an opportunity to deepen understanding of the data. Here are some strategies for dealing with this situation:

1. **Recognising and Documenting Contradictions**

• **Clear identification**: Make a careful note of contradictory information as it emerges. This keeps track of the different perspectives and opinions.
• **Context of contradictions**: Try to understand the context in which these contradictions arise. Sometimes differences of opinion can be linked to personal experiences or specific situations.

2. **Analysis of Contradictions**

• **Theming**: Group contradictory data under similar themes to see how they might fit together. This may reveal nuances and complexities you hadn't considered.
• **Pattern Analysis**: Look for recurring patterns in contradictions. Sometimes contradictions can emerge from the same theme, revealing opposing points of view on the same subject.

3. **Using Triangulation**

• **Multiple sources**: Compare contradictory data with other sources of information (such as statistics, previous studies, or other testimonies) to see if certain contradictions can be clarified or contextualised.
• **Various perspectives**: Involve other researchers or members of the team to discuss contradictions and gather a variety of viewpoints.

4. **Flexible coding**

• **Axial coding**: Use axial coding to link contradictory codes together. This can help structure the data to show how it complements or opposes each other.
• **Creating Nuanced Categories**: If contradictions frequently arise, consider creating categories that reflect this complexity, for example, by distinguishing between contexts or sub-groups.

5. **Critical interpretation**

- **Reflect on Bias**: Be aware of your own biases and prejudices. Think about how your perspective might influence the way you interpret contradictions.
- **Exploring Emotional Dimensions**: Consider the emotions and motivations behind contradictory data. This can provide additional insights into participants' feelings.

6. **Discussion and validation**

- **Feedback from participants**: If possible, share contradictions with participants to get their opinions. This can clarify points of view and enrich the analysis.
- **Discussion groups**: Organise discussions with colleagues or experts to explore contradictions and their significance.

7. **Transparent Report**

- **Inclusion of contradictions**: In your reports, mention contradictions and discuss them openly. This shows that you have taken into account the complexity of the data and reinforces the credibility of your analysis.
- **Nuanced conclusions**: Present conclusions that acknowledge contradictions and offer multiple interpretations, if necessary.

Dealing with conflicting data when coding qualitative data is a common challenge, but one that is essential to obtaining a thorough and nuanced analysis. Here are some strategies for addressing this issue:

1. **Recognising Contradiction**

- **Identifying inconsistencies**: Take note of any data that seems contradictory or does not align with existing codes or themes.
- **Documentation**: Record specific examples of contradictions for future reference.

2. **Revisiting the Coding Framework**

- **Code re-evaluation**: Review your code definitions and criteria to see if they need to be adjusted to better reflect the complexity of the data.
- **Create Sub-Categories**: If contradictions appear frequently, consider creating sub-categories to capture these nuances.

3. **Contextual analysis**

- **Context of the data**: Analyse the context in which the conflicting data was collected. Differences in situation, timing or participants can shed light on divergent perspectives.
- **Participants' perspectives**: Consider that contradictions may reflect different experiences or opinions, and that it is important to include these diverse voices.

4. **Data triangulation**

- **Cross-check with other sources**: Compare contradictory data with other sources of information (quantitative, qualitative, or previous studies) to better understand their significance.
- **Fact-checking**: If possible, validate contradictory information through additional research or interviews with participants.

5. **Team discussion**

- **Coding meetings**: Organise discussion sessions with other researchers or team members to debate contradictions and develop common interpretations.
- **Feedback and Collaboration**: Encourage an environment where team members can express their views and challenge interpretations.

6. **Theories and nuances**

- **Emerging theories**: Use contradictions as an opportunity to generate new hypotheses or theories that can enrich your understanding of the subject.

• **Acceptance of Complexity**: Recognise that contradictions can be an integral part of human reality and that they can enrich your analysis.

7. **Report on Contradictions**

• **Include in the Final Report**: When presenting your results, mention any contradictions and discuss their significance. This demonstrates rigorous analysis and a nuanced understanding of the data.
• **Practical implications**: Assess how these contradictions may influence future recommendations or actions.

A Museum of Computing and the Digital Society could become a key venue for exploring the evolution of digital technologies and their impact on our daily lives. Here are several key aspects to consider in its design and development:

1. **Permanent and temporary exhibitions**

• **History of Computing**: An interactive timeline of major innovations, from the first computers to smartphones, featuring iconic objects.
• **Emerging Technologies**: Exhibitions on artificial intelligence, augmented reality and other cutting-edge technologies that are shaping our future.
• **Social and Cultural Impact**: Sections dedicated to exploring the effects digital technologies on communication, work and culture.

2. **Interactive areas**

• **Hands-on workshops**: Areas where visitors can learn about programming, robotics and digital content creation.
• **Virtual Simulations**: Using virtual reality to offer immersive experiences, such as historical reconstructions of the evolution of computing.

3. **Education and awareness**

• **School Programmes**: Development of educational resources for schools, including guided tours and practical activities.

• **Conferences and Seminars**: Organisation of events with experts in the field to discuss current trends and future challenges.

4. **Digital preservation**

• **Archiving Digital Objects**: Creating a collection of digital artefacts, historical software and video games, preserving digital heritage.

• **Documentation and Accessibility**: Setting up an online database so that the public can explore the collections remotely.

5. **Partnerships and Collaborations**

• **Collaboration with universities**: Establishing partnerships with academic institutions for research and the development of educational programmes.

• **Partnerships with companies**: Working with technology companies on sponsored exhibitions and joint events.

6. **Use of Digital Media**

• **Virtual Visits**: Offer online visits to provide global access to the museum, particularly for those who cannot travel.

• **Mobile Applications**: Developing applications that enhance the visitor experience on site, with augmented reality features and audio guides.

7. **Impact Assessment**

• **Surveys and Feedback**: Collect feedback from visitors to improve exhibitions and programmes.

• **Data analysis**: Tracking online traffic and interactions to measure audience engagement and adjust offers accordingly.

A Museum of Computing and the Digital Society would be an exciting initiative, aimed at exploring the evolution of digital technologies and their impact on society. Here are some ideas for designing such a museum:

1. **Concept and Mission**

- **Objective**: To educate the public about the history of computing, technological innovations and their social, cultural and ethical implications.
- **Target audience**: Schools, students, researchers, IT professionals and the general public.

2. **Permanent Exhibitions**

- **History of Computing**: An interactive timeline of major advances, from the first computers to modern smartphones.
- **Evolution of the Internet**: Exhibitions on the birth of the web, browsers, social networks and cybersecurity issues.
- **Digital Art**: Showcasing works of art created using new technologies including multimedia installations.

3. **Temporary Exhibitions**

- **Current Themes**: Exploring contemporary issues such as artificial intelligence, virtual reality and emerging technologies.
- **Social Impact**: Analysing how technologies influence areas such as education, health and work.

4. **Interactive Installations**

- **Technology simulations**. giving visitors the chance to test software, program robots or experiment with virtual reality environments.
- **Practical workshops**: Offer coding sessions, hackathons or digital creation workshops.

5. **Education and awareness**

• **School Programmes**: Developing educational resources for teachers and students, including guided tours and educational activities.
• **Conferences and Round Tables**: Invite experts to discuss the ethical and social issues surrounding digital technologies.

6. **Partnerships and Collaborations**

• **Universities and schools**: Working with educational institutions to promote learning and research.
• **Technology companies**: Establish partnerships for events, exhibitions or mentoring programmes.

7. **Accessibility**

• **Virtual Tours**: Offering online experiences to reach a global audience and make the museum accessible to all.
• **Physical and digital accessibility**: Ensuring that facilities are accessible to people with disabilities.

8. **Assessment and Improvement**

• **Gathering Feedback**: Gathering visitors' impressions to improve exhibitions and programmes.
• **Impact analysis**: Assess how the museum influences visitors' understanding of and engagement with digital technologies.

XI. CONCLUSION

The ideas developed in this article are still only proposals and have not been validated by experience. They will be implemented in the coming months, during the construction of a first version of a virtual museum of computing. We are aware of the difficulties of this undertaking, which seem to us to be of two kinds.

- Conceptual difficulties. The choice of the inductive approach (starting from known applications and objects to introduce scientific concepts) is a gamble. The definition of the different stages and the way in which they are linked will undoubtedly need to be fine-tuned after evaluation. Finally, as in any popularisation approach, a balance will have to be maintained between scientific rigour and didactic simplification.
- Practical difficulties. The presentation of the examples will have to be sufficiently attractive not to discourage further visits. This implies rigorous planning of the layout of the examples and the progression of the explanations, in particular through the well thought-out use of visual and auditory aids. We will need the help of specialists in these techniques.

We believe that our approach is original, because existing virtual museums for computing are essentially based around collections of objects, with presentations focusing mainly on technical aspects. On the other hand, there are presentations of the scientific concepts of computing, but they are not generally aimed at the general public. Once we have produced a first version of our presentation, we plan to try it out with a variety of audiences: high school pupils, students, the general public, IT professionals, in collaboration with specialists in cultural and scientific outreach. This will enable us to assess the relevance of our approach and gather information that will enable us to improve it.

REFERENCES

Aconit (2012). Towards a virtual museum of computing, Colloquium "Towards a Museum of Computing and the Digital Society in France?", Paris, November 2012.

Dowek G. (2011). The four concepts of computing, Didapro 4, October 2011. See https://who.rocq.inria.fr/Gilles.Dowek/philo.html

Dowek G. (2012). Computing in the classification of sciences. Seminar "Philosophie de l'informatique, de la logique et de leurs interfaces", École normale supérieure, 30 January 2012. See https://who.rocq.inria.fr/Gilles.Dowek/philo.html

Wing J. (2008). La pensée informatique, Bulletin Specif n° 60, December 2008. See http://www.specif.org/bulletins/specif060.pdf

THE AUTHOR

Ryaz Jeancy NGOVULA MBISI *is an Assistant at the Institut Supérieur des Techniques Médicales de Kikwit (ISTM KKT). He conducts research in the field of operating systems, software engineering and distributed systems and applications, in the areas of statistics. He is currently interested in the history of computing and its popularisation in statistics.*

TABLE OF CONTENTS

MIX
Papier aus verantwortungsvollen Quellen
Paper from responsible sources
FSC® C105338

Printed by Books on Demand GmbH, Norderstedt / Germany